COOK'S NOTES

These recipes are for the family to enjoy making together. Some could be dangerous without the help of an adult. Children, please **ALWAYS** have an adult with you when you are using knives, handling anything hot, or using a food processor or blender.

For Olivia and Lorina, who both
died as a result of neurological problems. I hope the royalties
from this book will help others. F.D.

For Judith, with love; and for the
Neurology unit of Dundee Royal Infirmary. Q.B.

ACKNOWLEDGMENTS

On behalf of the Roald Dahl Foundation, I wish to thank Quentin Blake for making this book possible by filling it with a feast of visual humor. A big thank you also to Josie Fison for inventing the wondercrump Revolting Recipes; Jan Baldwin, for her ingenious photography; Wendy Kress and Linda Ambrose for doing the typing while being force-fed the samples and suffering from constant indigestion; my editors, Tom Maschler, Melissa Jones and Clare Conville, and our designer Paul Welti for their constant faith in me. Last and by no means least, I thank Roald, my fantastic husband, without whose inspiration this book would never have happened.

Felicity Dahl, CHAIRMAN, THE ROALD DAHL FOUNDATION.

PUFFIN BOOKS
Published by the Penguin Group
Penguin Books USA Inc., 375 Hudson Street, New York, New York 10014, U.S.A.
Penguin Books Ltd, 27 Wrights Lane, London W8 5TZ, England
Penguin Books Australia Ltd, Ringwood, Victoria, Australia
Penguin Books Canada Ltd, 10 Alcorn Avenue, Toronto, Ontario, Canada M4V 3B2
Penguin Books (N.Z.) Ltd, 182-190 Wairau Road, Auckland 10, New Zealand

Penguin Books Ltd, Registered Offices: Harmondsworth, Middlesex, England

First published in Great Britain by Jonathan Cape Ltd,
a division of Random House, 1994
First published in the United States of America by Viking Children's Books,
a division of Penguin Books USA Inc., 1994
Published in Puffin Books, 1997

7 9 10 8

Text copyright © Felicity Dahl and the executors of the Estate of Roald Dahl, 1994
Illustrations copyright © Quentin Blake, 1994
Photographs copyright © Jan Baldwin, 1994
All rights reserved

THE LIBRARY OF CONGRESS HAS CATALOGED THE VIKING EDITION UNDER
CATALOG CARD NUMBER: 94-76366

Puffin Books ISBN 0-14-037820-0

Printed in Singapore

Roald Dahl's
REVOLTING RECIPES

Illustrated by Quentin Blake
with photographs by Jan Baldwin
Recipes compiled by Josie Fison
and Felicity Dahl

PUFFIN BOOKS

RECIPE LIST

INTRODUCTION

TREATS

Treats were an essential part of Roald's life—never too many, never too few, and always perfectly timed. He made you feel like a king receiving the finest gift in the land.

A treat could be a wine gum lifted silently in the middle of the night out of a large sweet jar kept permanently by his bedside. It could be a lobster and oyster feast placed on the table after a secret visit to the fishmonger, his favorite shop. It could be the first new potato, broad bean, or lettuce from the garden, a basket of field mushrooms, or a superb conker. A different kind of treat would be an unannounced visit to a school, causing chaos to teachers and, I suspect, a great deal of fun for the children.

Just before Roald died, while we were writing a book about food we loved and happy memories, it was suggested we should write a book for children, based on the many wonderful and varied foods that appear in his books. Roald buried his face in his hands and gasped, "Oh no, Liccy, the work! The thought daunts me."

A few weeks later there, sitting on my blotter, was a pile of papers neatly clipped together, listing every food from Willy Wonka's Nutty Crunch Surprise to the mound of mysterious spare ribs consumed by Hansel and Gretel in *Rhyme Stew*. On top was a note saying, "It's a great idea, but God knows how you will do it."

Well, I *have* done it. *Revolting Recipes* is an interpretation of some of the scrumptious and wonderfully disgusting dishes that appear in Roald's books. Quentin Blake's part in all this is without parallel, and his wickedly funny illustrations together with Jan Baldwin's skillful photographs and Josie Fison's interpretation make this book the *ultimate* treat.

Felicity Dahl, GIPSY HOUSE 1994

STRAWBERRY-FLAVORED CHOCOLATE-COATED FUDGE

FROM *CHARLIE AND THE CHOCOLATE FACTORY*

MAKES ENOUGH FOR 10 GREEDY CHILDREN

YOU WILL NEED:

8 x 10 inch shallow baking pan
large heavy-bottomed saucepan
wax paper
candy thermometer (optional)

2 cups sugar
1 stick unsalted butter
4 ounces evaporated milk
2 ounces strawberry syrup
* (Hershey's, if available)*
4 ounces melted semisweet
* chocolate for*
* dipping*

1. Line an 8 x 10 inch shallow baking pan with buttered wax paper.

2. Put the sugar, butter, evaporated milk, and strawberry syrup into a large heavy-bottomed saucepan and place over low heat.

3. Stir occasionally. Once the sugar has dissolved, bring the mixture to a boil gently, stirring constantly to prevent sticking and burning on the bottom of the pan. Boil gently until a little of the mixture dropped into cold water forms a soft ball, about 5 minutes. (Or you

can place a warmed candy thermometer in the saucepan and boil the mixture until it reaches 234°F.)

4. Take the pan off the heat and stir until the bubbles subside.

5. Beat rapidly with a wooden spoon until the mixture thickens and becomes granular, about 3 minutes.

6. Pour the fudge into the lined baking pan and let set. If necessary, smooth with a spatula dipped in boiling water.

7. With shaped cutters, cut out the fudge, and dip one side into the melted chocolate; or decorate with piped chocolate, creating different patterns, as in the illustration.

SERVES 4 TO 5

YOU WILL NEED:

large saucepan
blender or food processor
sieve

2 tablespoons (¼ stick) unsalted
  butter
12 scallions, coarsely chopped
1 small potato, diced
1 clove garlic, crushed
12 ounces frozen peas
3 ¾ cups chicken stock
salt and pepper

GARNISH:

6 ounces frozen peas
5 ounces heavy cream

GREEN PEA SOUP
FROM *THE WITCHES*

1. Melt the butter in a large saucepan.

2. Add the scallions, potato, and garlic.

3. Cover with a lid and cook over low heat for 10 minutes.

4. Add the peas, stock, and a pinch each of salt and pepper. Bring to a boil and simmer slowly for about 15 minutes.

5. Remove from the heat and purée until liquefied.

6. Pass through a sieve into a clean saucepan.

7. Reheat, adding the peas to garnish. Cook until the peas are just tender, add the cream, and heat through. Season to taste with more salt and pepper if necessary.

WORMY SPAGHETTI
FROM *THE TWITS*

SERVES 4 TO 5

YOU WILL NEED:

medium saucepan
large saucepan

SAUCE:

3 tablespoons olive oil
1 onion, chopped
2 stalks of celery, chopped
 (optional)
1 clove garlic, crushed
14 ounces canned plum tomatoes
1 tablespoon tomato paste
1 tablespoon chopped fresh
 parsley
1 bay leaf
1 teaspoon sugar
2 carrots, grated
salt and pepper

2 ounces fusilli
8 ounces tricolor spaghetti (2
 ounces spinach, 2 ounces
 whole-wheat, and 4 ounces
 regular spaghetti)
6 ounces Cheddar cheese

1. Heat 2 tablespoons of oil in a medium saucepan and cook the onion, celery, and garlic over low heat, covered, until soft.

2. Add the remaining ingredients for the sauce *except* the carrots. Bring to a boil and simmer for 30 minutes.

3. Remove the bay leaf and purée the sauce until liquefied. Return the sauce to the saucepan, season with salt and pepper to taste, and keep warm.

4. Meanwhile, bring a large saucepan of water to a boil and add a tablespoon of oil and a pinch of salt. Break the fusilli and the tricolor spaghetti into thirds and cook until *al dente,* about 5 to 10 minutes.

5. Fold the grated carrots into the sauce and heat through.

6. Serve the spaghetti on individual plates, topped with the sauce and grated cheese.

SNOZZCUMBERS

FROM *THE BFG*

SERVES 8

YOU WILL NEED:

vegetable peeler
melon scoop (optional) or tea-
spoon
paintbrush

2 large cucumbers
1 can (3 ¼ ounces) tuna
1 to 2 tomatoes, deseeded and
chopped
3 cocktail gherkins, finely
chopped
3 tablespoons mayonnaise
2 teaspoons poppy seeds
salt and pepper

COATING:

a little extra mayonnaise
popcorn (cheese-flavored popcorn
tastes best)
extra poppy seeds

1. Peel the cucumbers.

2. With the pointed end of the vegetable peeler, cut several grooves down the length of each cucumber and carefully scoop out little holes at random between the grooves.

3. Cut off the ends of the cucumbers about 1½ inches from each end.

4. Hollow out the seeds from the body of the cucumbers using a melon scoop or a teaspoon.

5. Stand each cucumber in a tall glass and allow the excess liquids to drain (about 30 minutes).

6. Thoroughly drain the tuna and mix in the chopped tomatoes, gherkins, mayonnaise, and poppy seeds. Season to taste with salt and pepper.

7. Using a teaspoon, fill the cucumbers with the tuna mixture, packing it down with the handle of the spoon.

8. Paint a little mayonnaise in the grooves on the outside of the cucumbers and carefully fill the grooves with poppy seeds. (A steady hand is useful!)

9. Place a small piece of popcorn in each hole between the grooves, putting a little mayonnaise in first to

secure the popcorn. These can also be coated in poppy seeds if you wish.

10. Replace the cucumber ends.

Sophie said the original Snozzcumber tasted of frogskin and rotten fish. The BFG said it tasted like cockroaches and slime wanglers. What do you think?

FRESH MUDBURGERS
FROM *JAMES AND THE GIANT PEACH*

MAKES 10 MUDBURGERS

YOU WILL NEED:

mixing bowl
grill or nonstick skillet

1 ½ pounds ground beef
1 medium onion, chopped
3 tablespoons tomato paste
2 tablespoons Dijon mustard
1 tablespoon Worcestershire
  sauce
2 to 3 tablespoons capers,
  drained
¼ cup chopped fresh parsley
salt and pepper
1 egg, beaten
relish (optional)

1. In a mixing bowl, break up the ground beef.

2. Add all the ingredients except the egg and gently mix together.

3. Add the egg, mix thoroughly, and pat into mudburgers.

4. Preheat the grill and grill for 4-5 minutes on each side, or fry in a nonstick skillet.

5. Serve in a bun with a "revolting" garnish. Relish is ideal!

ONION RINGS
(TO GO WITH MUDBURGERS)

YOU WILL NEED:

large plastic bag

1 onion
flour seasoned with salt and
  pepper
vegetable oil
salt

1. Peel the onion and cut into ⅛-inch-thick slices, against the grain. Separate the rings.

2. Put them in a large plastic bag containing seasoned flour, and shake until the rings are lightly coated with the flour. Shake off any excess.

3. Deep-fry in hot oil until crisp and golden.

MOSQUITOES' TOES AND WAMPFISH ROES MOST DELICATELY FRIED

FROM *JAMES AND THE GIANT PEACH*

SERVES 18

YOU WILL NEED:

food processor
plastic wrap
wax paper
skillet

8 ounces fresh cod fillets
2 tablespoons finely grated fresh
*   ginger*
10 scallions, coarsely chopped
½ tablespoon cornstarch
salt and pepper
1 egg white
6 to 8 slices white bread
sesame seeds
poppy seeds
vegetable oil, enough to come ¼
*   inch up the side of the skillet*

These need to be refrigerated for 30 minutes before frying, so pre-pare ahead.

1. In a food processor, quickly blend together the cod, ginger, scallions, cornstarch, and a pinch each of salt and pepper.

2. With the motor running, add the egg white until just combined.

3. Cut the crusts off the bread. Spread the fish mixture in a thick layer on the bread slices.

4. Sprinkle generously with sesame and poppy seeds. Pat the seeds into the fish mixture with the flat side of a knife.

5. Cut each slice of bread into three equal strips.

6. Place on a plate with a sheet of wax paper between each layer. Cover with plastic wrap and refrigerate for 30 minutes.

7. Heat the oil in the skillet until hot, and fry the bread slices, seed side down, until golden brown. Turn over and repeat.

8. Drain on paper towels before serving.

BIRD PIE
FROM *THE TWITS*

SERVES 4 TO 6

YOU WILL NEED:

large saucepan
blackbird (a black pastry funnel
  found in specialty cooks' shops
  and mail order catalogs)
9-inch pie dish
rolling pin

¼ cup pearl barley
2 tablespoons unsalted butter
1 onion, finely chopped
1 pound turkey breast, cut into
  thin strips
12 ounces pork sausage meat
2 tablespoons chopped fresh sage
  (optional)

1. Simmer the pearl barley in water for about 20 minutes, or until soft.

2. In a large saucepan melt the butter and gently fry the onion until soft. Add the turkey strips and fry quickly until golden.

3. Remove the saucepan from the heat and add the sausage meat. Mix well.

4. Add the sage (if using), sour cream, yogurt, cornstarch mixture, chicken stock, and beaten egg. Season to taste with salt and pepper and mix thoroughly.

5. Place the blackbird in the middle of the pie dish. Surround with the turkey mixture. Sprinkle on the chopped ham, followed by the chopped egg.

6. Preheat the oven to 400°F.

5 ounces sour cream

5 ounces plain yogurt

1 level teaspoon cornstarch, mixed with 1 teaspoon cold water

½ cup chicken stock

2 eggs, one beaten, one hard-boiled and chopped

salt and pepper

2 ounces ham, chopped

9 ounces ready-made puff pastry or instant biscuit dough

1 egg yolk

8 parsley sprigs with the leaves pinched off or colored pipe cleaners

7. Roll out the pastry to a circle ⅛ inch thick. Make sure it is at least one inch wider than the pie dish all the way around.

8. Cut the extra one inch from the pastry in one long circular strip (it should be slightly larger than the rim of the pie dish). Brush the pie dish rim with egg yolk, press the pastry strip down onto the rim, and brush the strip with egg yolk.

9. Lift the remaining pastry carefully (you can drape it over the rolling pin) and lay it over the turkey mixture. Cut a slit in the center and ease the blackbird's beak through the pastry, taking care not to stretch it. Press the pastry down firmly along the rim and cut away any excess. Use a fork to crimp the edge.

10. Glaze the pastry with egg yolk and scatter the pearl barley on top. Form a "worm" out of a strip of pastry, glaze it with egg yolk, and place it inside the bird's beak.

11. Refrigerate the pie for ten minutes.

12. Bake for 30 to 40 minutes, or until the pastry is well risen and golden brown.

13. Stick the stripped parsley stalks, or folded pipe cleaners, in pairs into the pastry crust to look like birds' legs. If you like, singe the ends to look like toes.

BUNCE'S DOUGHNUTS

FROM *FANTASTIC MR. FOX*

MAKES 12 TO 14

YOU WILL NEED:

food processor (optional)
plastic wrap
rolling pin
two round cookie cutters, 1 ¼
   inches and 2 ½ inches
large bowl

½ cup light brown sugar, firmly
   packed
4 tablespoons unsalted butter
1 egg, lightly beaten
1 pound all-purpose flour
½ tablespoon baking powder
½ teaspoon cinnamon
a large pinch of salt
2 tablespoons hot water
¼ teaspoon vanilla extract
½ cup milk
vegetable oil for deep frying
sugar for coating

These are best eaten warm. The dough needs to be made and refrigerated for at least two hours before cooking, and will keep overnight in the refrigerator.

1. Cream the brown sugar and butter until pale and creamy—this can be done using a food processor.

2. Gradually add the egg until blended.

3. Add the remaining ingredients. The dough should be fairly stiff but smooth.

4. Cover with plastic wrap and refrigerate for 2 hours.

5. Divide the dough in half and return one half to the refrigerator.

6. On a floured surface roll out the other half of the dough to a quarter-inch thick. With the cutters cut out as many doughnuts as possible, using the larger one to cut the doughnut shape and the smaller one to make the hole.

7. Gather up the scraps and roll and cut out as many additional doughnuts as possible. Repeat the rolling and cutting with the remaining half of the dough.

8. Heat the vegetable oil to 375°F.

9. Fry the doughnuts in small batches, turning once, until deep golden brown.

10. Drain on paper towels.

11. Put the sugar in a bowl and add a few doughnuts at a time, shaking them in the sugar until coated. Serve immediately.

THE ENORMOUS CROCODILE

Steps 1 to 7 should be done the day before serving.

1. Slice one end of the baguette horizontally in half along one third of its length to make the mouth.

MAKES ONE CENTER-
PIECE TO NIBBLE AT

YOU WILL NEED:

*wire coat hanger with the hook
    cut off (optional)*
toothpicks
*1 tube (4 ½ ounces) white deco-
    rating icing*
long tray or board

THE CROCODILE:

1 large baguette (body)
*3 ½ ounces whole blanched
    almonds (teeth)*
*1 package (10 ounces) frozen
    chopped spinach (skin)*
2 globe artichokes (scales)
1 slice ham (tongue)
1 egg, hard-boiled (eyeballs)
1 black olive (pupils)
4 cooked sausages (legs)
12 cocktail gherkins (toes)

2. Now slice the other end horizontally to make the body, leaving ½ to ¾ inch unsliced between the body and the mouth (this is the neck). Carefully lift off the top of the body section.

3. Hollow out the top and bottom of the body, and the lower jaw, leaving a wide border for the lower lip.

4. Fold the coat hanger in half (having previously removed the hook), and carefully place it inside the mouth to prop up the jaws.

5. Defrost, drain, and cook the spinach. Set aside.

6. Boil the artichokes for 30 to 40 minutes, drain, and set aside. When cold, pluck the leaves (reserving the hairy choke and heart as a treat for adults later!).

EGG FILLING:

(quantities depend on the size of the baguette)
6 to 8 eggs, hard-boiled
salt and pepper
3 to 4 tablespoons mayonnaise
1 small bunch watercress, leaves only, chopped

7. EGG FILLING: Finely chop the 6 to 8 hard-boiled eggs, and season to taste with salt and pepper. Mix in the mayonnaise and watercress and spoon into the body.

8. TONGUE AND TEETH: Place the tongue in the mouth, and insert the teeth (almonds) into the border of the upper and lower lips. Secure any loose teeth with the decorating icing.

9. SKIN AND SCALES: Spread the cooked spinach over the head and body. Mold the mixture to look like scaly skin. Position artichoke leaves as shown.

10. EYES: Cut the hard-boiled egg in half and turn the egg yolks around so that they protrude. Add the pupils (half-olives). Secure with toothpicks.

NOTE: IMPORTANT
This recipe is designed to create a centerpiece for a party or other special occasion. If you wish to eat the croc, simply follow the recipe but do not insert the coat hanger. His jaws will be closed, but he'll still be delicious!

Warn children that there are sharp toothpicks in the crocodile's eyes and legs.

11. LEGS AND TOES: Slice the sausages in half and position for legs. Hold in place with toothpicks. Add the cocktail gherkins for toes.

GEORGE'S MARVELOUS
MEDICINE CHICKEN SOUP

SERVES 6

YOU WILL NEED:

large saucepan

2 small or 1 large chicken (total: 5 to 6 pounds)
4 small onions
4 ounces mushrooms
3 large carrots
2 leeks
1 tablespoon chopped fresh tarragon or 1 teaspoon dried tarragon
salt and pepper

If you want to serve this for lunch, you will need to make it the day before.

1. Quarter the chicken(s) and chop 2 of the onions. Place the chicken and chopped onions in a large saucepan and cover with water.

2. Bring to a boil and simmer until the liquid has reduced by half. Skim the surface when necessary. Cover the chicken with more water and reduce by half again. This takes at least 4 hours. Cool.

3. Strain the liquid and set it aside—you should have about 6 or 7 cups.

4. Pick the chicken meat off the bones, chop it, and set it aside.

5. Chop the remaining onions and other vegetables, add to the stock with the tarragon, and cook until tender.

6. Season with salt and pepper to taste. Add the chicken meat, heat through, and serve.

KROKAN ICE CREAM

FROM *BOY*

SERVES 4–6

YOU WILL NEED:

aluminum foil
baking sheet
skillet
rolling pin
plastic bag

2 tablespoons butter
3 ounces almonds, skinned and
*   coarsely chopped*
²/₃ cup sugar
1 quart good-quality vanilla ice
*   cream*

"Krokan" is the Norwegian word for a delicious burned toffee mixture. The ice cream will keep for a couple of days before the Krokan begins to go soft.

1. Make the Krokan first. Lightly grease a piece of aluminum foil placed on a baking sheet.

2. Mix the butter, chopped almonds, and sugar in a heavy skillet.

3. Place over moderate heat and cook, stirring constantly and taking care that the mixture doesn't burn.

4. When it's a good golden color, pour the mixture onto the greased aluminum foil.

5. Allow the Krokan to cool completely.

6. When it is cool, place it in a plastic bag and lightly crush it into small pieces by rolling over it with a rolling pin.

7. Let the ice cream soften at room temperature and then stir in the crushed Krokan until thoroughly mixed.

8. Place the ice cream mixture back in the freezer until it's frozen again.

TOFFEE-APPLE TREES

FROM *CHARLIE AND THE CHOCOLATE FACTORY*

SERVES 4

YOU WILL NEED:

melon scoop
manicure sticks (available at the
    drugstore) or short skewers
small saucepan
candy thermometer (optional)
8-inch bowl containing water
    and ice cubes
aluminum foil

4 eating apples
¹/₂ tablespoon water
¹/₂ cup plus 1 tablespoon sugar
2 tablespoons butter

These need to be made at the last moment because they will start to melt after an hour.

1. Using the melon scoop, scoop out as many balls as possible from two apples. Each apple ball must have some skin on it. Push a manicure stick or skewer into each ball through the remaining skin.

2. To make the toffee: Place the water, sugar, butter, and candy thermometer (if using) in the saucepan and heat over very low heat, stirring occasionally, until the sugar dissolves. Turn up the heat and boil until the mixture becomes a deep chestnut brown, about 25 minutes or when the temperature reaches 320°F. Turn off

the heat and allow the bubbles to subside.

3. Remove the bowl of ice water from the refrigerator. Working as quickly as possible, dip the apples into the toffee one at a time. Rotate a few times to get an even coating and drop into the bowl of ice water for 30 seconds. Do not dry the baby toffee apples; stick them directly into the remaining whole apples.

HOT FROGS

FROM *JAMES AND THE GIANT PEACH*

SERVES 6 TO 7

YOU WILL NEED:

pencil
cardboard
scissors
rolling pin
baking sheet
pastry brush

9 ounces ready-made puff pastry
*   or instant biscuit dough*
3 to 4 medium-sized Granny
*   Smith apples (when cut in*
*   half they should fit inside the*
*   pattern)*
6 ounces raisins soaked in
*   orange juice*

Soak the raisins in the orange juice for a couple of hours before beginning this recipe.

1. Draw a frog measuring about 5 × 5 inches on the cardboard, and cut it out to use as a pattern.

2. Preheat oven to 400°F.

3. Roll out the pastry to a thickness of ⅛ inch.

4. With your pattern, cut out as many frogs as possible, about 6 or 7.

5. With a fork, gently prick each frog's middle several times.

6. Cut the apples in half vertically.

7. With a melon scoop or teaspoon, scoop out the apple cores and seeds.

1 egg yolk
1 tablespoon milk
12 to 14 raisins soaked in
  orange juice (eyes)
6 small containers ready-to-eat
  vanilla pudding (4 ounces
  each)
green food coloring

8. Fill each apple hollow with a generous teaspoon of the orange-soaked raisins.

9. Lightly beat the egg yolk together with the milk. Using a pastry brush, brush each frog with a little of the mixture.

10. Place the apples, cut side down, on the back of each frog.

11. Position the frogs' eyes using the 12 or 14 raisins.

12. Lightly dust a baking sheet with flour and place the frogs on it.

13. Bake for about 15 to 20 minutes, or until the pastry is risen and golden in color.

14. Mix a few drops of food coloring into the pudding, and serve each frog on top of a pool of green pudding.

MR. TWIT'S BEARD FOOD
FROM *THE TWITS*

SERVES 4

YOU WILL NEED:

small saucepan
skillet
large oval plate

2 large potatoes
a chunk of butter
a little milk
8 cocktail franks
4 mushrooms, 2 for the nose and
    2 for the ears (oyster mush-
    rooms are good for the ears if
    you can find them)
1 hard-boiled egg

1. Peel the potatoes, and cook in boiling water until soft. Drain and mash with the butter and milk.

2. Brown the franks in a skillet.

TO ASSEMBLE MR. TWIT'S FACE:

3. With about a third of the mashed potatoes, form a base for his face.

4. EYES: Peel the hard-boiled egg and cut in half. Remove the yolk halves (taking care to keep them from crumbling), and place them upside down on the egg whites. Cut the olive in half and use the halves as pupils.

5. EYEBROWS: Cut his eyebrows from the toast. (Cut them out in one continuous strip, so his eyebrows join in the middle).

1 black olive
2 slices white bread (one of
   them toasted)
1 small bag shoestring potato
   sticks
1 small bag pretzel sticks
$^1/_4$ cup peas
$^1/_4$ cup baked beans
a handful of cornflakes
ketchup
4 ounces Swiss cheese, cubed
$^1/_2$ cup brown gravy (optional)

6. NOSE: Carefully separate the mushroom caps from the stems. Form the nose out of a stem, with two upside-down caps as nostrils.

7. EARS: Use one mushroom for each ear.

8. HAIR AND BEARD: With the remaining mashed potatoes, form a base for his hair and beard.

9. MOUTH: Slice three franks in half vertically, leaving an uncut end on two of the franks for the corners of his mouth. Join together into a mouth shape.

10. TEETH: Break the slice of white bread into tiny pieces without any crust. Roll and press them between your fingers into tooth shapes and position in his mouth.

11. BEARD: Build up his beard out of the shoestring potato sticks (bristles), and the remaining franks (cut into little pieces), pretzel sticks, peas, baked beans, cornflakes, and ketchup.

12. To warm up, preheat the oven to 350°F and heat Mr. Twit for about 10 to 15 minutes, or microwave (check manufacturer's instructions).

13. Sprinkle the cheese cubes on his beard. Serve with gravy if you wish.

LICKABLE WALLPAPER
FROM *CHARLIE AND THE CHOCOLATE FACTORY*

This wallpaper needs to be made a day or two before serving to allow it to dry out. It will keep easily for a week and can be rolled up for storage.

APPLE WALLPAPER:

MAKES 6 STRIPS

YOU WILL NEED:

food processor
small Pyrex bowl
small saucepan
plastic wrap
rolling pin
wire rack

5 ounces dried apple chunks
½ tablespoon light brown sugar
2 tablespoons water
1 teaspoon gelatin

APRICOT WALLPAPER

This is also delicious. Simply substitute 5 ounces dried apricots for the dried apples, omit all other ingredients, and skip steps 2 and 3.

1. In a food processor, purée the apple chunks with the brown sugar until the mixture resembles chopped nuts.

2. Put the water in a small Pyrex bowl and sprinkle in the gelatin. Let stand for 5 minutes, then set the bowl in a small saucepan filled with a little simmering water and let the gelatin dissolve.

3. Once the gelatin has dissolved, slowly add it to the apple purée and mix well.

4. Shape the purée into a ball and place it on a large sheet of plastic wrap. Gently flatten it with your hand into a square shape.

5. Now place another sheet of plastic wrap on top and gently roll out the purée into a thin squarish sheet about 1/16 of an inch thick (you should be able to see through it when it is held up to the light).

6. Rest the wallpaper on a wire rack and carefully remove the top sheet of plastic wrap. Let stand in a warm place to dry out.

7. After eight hours or so turn the wallpaper over, gently remove the bottom sheet of plastic wrap, and let dry again.

8. To decorate, cut each sheet of fruit into long strips of equal width and decorate with fresh fruit, melted chocolate, icing, edible flowers, etc. (see illustration).

CANDY-COATED PENCILS FOR SUCKING IN CLASS

FROM *CHARLIE AND THE CHOCOLATE FACTORY*

MAKES 6

YOU WILL NEED:

6 pencils
Play-Doh, Plasticine, or model-
ing clay
candy thermometer (optional)
buttered 8 x 10 inch baking
pan lined with wax paper
buttered knife

½ pound sugar cubes
½ cup plus 2 tablespoons water
a good pinch of cream of tartar
a few drops of flavoring and col-
oring

1. Put the sugar and water in a pan over low heat and stir until the sugar has dissolved.

2. Raise the heat. When the syrup is almost boiling, add the cream of tartar, and insert a warmed candy thermometer (if using).

3. Boil without stirring to 250°F, or until a little of the syrup dropped into cold water forms a hard ball (a ball that will hold its shape but is still pliable).

4. Remove from the heat and add flavoring and coloring. Do not overstir and *be very careful,* as the mixture is extremely hot.

5. Pour the mixture into the lined baking pan. The edges of the mixture will cool more quickly than the center, so as the mixture cools, turn the edges inward with a buttered knife, but *do not stir.*

6. Working quickly, lay two-thirds of a pencil (not the point end) on top of the mixture. Using the buttered knife, lift up the candy and gently wrap it around the pencil. You can create all sorts of shapes before it

hardens. When the candy is almost set, stand your pencil point end down in the Play-Doh. Try not to put your fingers on the candy coating, as you will leave your fingerprints behind.

7. Repeat step 6 with the other pencils.

NOTE: Do not double the recipe to make more; make several batches instead.

HANSEL AND GRETEL
SPARE RIBS

FROM *RHYME STEW*

SERVES 4

YOU WILL NEED:

roasting pan

1 tablespoon Worcestershire
   sauce
1 tablespoon soy sauce
1 tablespoon mustard
1 tablespoon ketchup
1 tablespoon honey
1 medium onion, finely chopped
salt and pepper
1 ½ pounds spare ribs

1. Preheat the oven to 425°F.

2. Place the ribs in a roasting pan.

3. Mix all the remaining ingredients together and spread the mixture on the ribs with a knife.

4. Place the pan of ribs in the oven and bake for about 1 ½ hours, turning them over every half hour and basting them with the juices.

NOTE: These must be well cooked and crunchy, as in the picture.

BUTTERSCOTCH

FROM *CHARLIE AND THE CHOCOLATE FACTORY*

MAKES ABOUT 3 CUPS
(3 TO 4 MUGS)

YOU WILL NEED:

small saucepan
large bowl

2 tablespoons butter
2 tablespoons sugar
1 ounce light corn syrup
2 ½ cups skim milk
3 ounces plain yogurt

1. In a saucepan over low heat, melt together the butter, sugar, and corn syrup, stirring constantly, until the sugar has dissolved (about 10 minutes). Add a little milk to the pan, about ¼ cup, then transfer to a bowl.

2. Whisk in a little more milk, followed by all the yogurt.

3. Whisk in the remaining milk.

4. Cover with plastic wrap. Chill before serving.

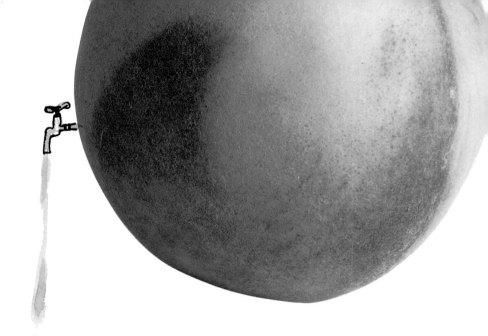

SERVES 4 TO 6

YOU WILL NEED:

blender or food processor

1 can (16 ounces) peaches in
    fruit juice
1 can (5 ounces) mangos
juice of 1 lemon

OR

6 fresh peaches, skinned and
    pitted
half a mango
juice of 1 lemon

PEACH JUICE
FROM *JAMES AND THE GIANT PEACH*

1. Purée all ingredients until liquefied. Add ice
cubes and serve immediately.

STINK BUGS' EGGS

FROM *JAMES AND THE GIANT PEACH*

SERVES 4

YOU WILL NEED:

saucepan
bowl

4 eggs
3 to 4 brown outer onion skins
*   or 1 tablespoon food coloring*

These need to be made a day in advance and can be dyed naturally or with food coloring.

1. Place the eggs in a saucepan filled with water and bring to a boil.

2. Turn down the heat and gently simmer for 10 minutes. Take off the heat, cool in cold water (this is important), and then drain.

3. Carefully crack the shells all over with the back of a spoon (without breaking off any shell). Then color the eggs with either of the following methods.

NATURAL COLORING METHOD:

Put the onion skins in the saucepan, lay the cracked, hard-boiled eggs on top, and cover with water. Bring

mayonnaise
salt and pepper
one or more of the following:
  chopped ham, grated cheese,
  cream cheese, chopped
  gherkins, Worcestershire
  sauce, curry powder, tomato
  sauce, cayenne pepper
2 carrots, grated
1 bunch of watercress, large
  stems removed
grated Parmesan cheese or
  asafetida (optional)

to a boil and simmer about 1 hour, or until the liquid is a deep brown color. Check now and then to be sure the water is not boiling away. Remove from heat.

FOOD COLORING METHOD:

Place the eggs in a bowl, cover with water, and add about 1 tablespoon of food coloring.

4. Let stand for at least 8 hours or overnight.

5. Remove the shells and cut the eggs in half lengthwise. Carefully remove the yolks, mash them with a fork, and mix with a little mayonnaise and salt and pepper.

6. The egg yolks can be mixed with your choice from the following: chopped ham, grated cheese, cream cheese, chopped gherkins, Worcestershire sauce, curry powder, tomato sauce, or cayenne pepper.

7. Replace the egg yolk mixture in the egg white halves and serve on a nest of watercress and grated carrot.

NOTE: If you want to make the eggs very smelly, sprinkle with grated Parmesan cheese—or with asafetida (obtainable from specialist Indian shops), which smells like sweaty socks!

BRUCE BOGTROTTER'S CAKE

FROM *MATILDA*

YOU WILL NEED:

8 ½-inch round cake pan
wax paper
Pyrex bowl
large mixing bowl
saucepan
wire rack

8 ounces good-quality semisweet
*   chocolate*
1 ½ sticks (12 tablespoons)
*   unsalted butter, softened*
1 cup plus 2 tablespoons sugar
¼ cup all-purpose flour
6 eggs, separated, yolks lightly
*   beaten*

1. Preheat the oven to 350°F.

2. Line the cake pan with wax paper and butter the bottom and sides of the paper.

3. Melt the chocolate in a Pyrex bowl set in a saucepan of simmering water or in a microwave on low heat. Mix in the butter and stir until melted.

4. Transfer to a large bowl and add the sugar, flour, and lightly beaten egg yolks.

5. Whisk the egg whites until stiff. Gently fold half of the whites into the chocolate mixture, blending thoroughly, then fold in the remaining whites.

6. Pour the batter into the cake pan and bake for about 35 minutes. There will be a thin crust on top of the cake, and if tested with a toothpick the inside will appear undercooked (don't worry, the cake will get

ICING:

*8 ounces good-quality semisweet
  chocolate*
8 ounces heavy cream

firmer as it cools). Remove from the oven, and let cool in the pan on a wire rack.

7. While the cake is cooling, make the icing. Melt the chocolate with the cream in a heavy-bottomed saucepan over lowest heat, stirring occasionally until the chocolate is fully melted and blended with the cream. Remove from heat and let cool slightly.

8. When the cake is cool enough to handle, remove it from the pan and discard the wax paper. The cake is prone to sinking slightly in the middle so flip it upside down before icing by placing a plate on top and carefully turning over the cake pan and plate together.

9. Carefully spread the chocolate icing all over the cake with a spatula.

45

SCRAMBLED DREGS

FROM *JAMES AND THE GIANT PEACH*

SERVES 2

YOU WILL NEED:

saucepan

*2 tablespoons (¼ stick) unsalted
    butter*
2 eggs, lightly beaten
*14 ounces canned chicken con-
    sommé*
salt and pepper

1. Melt the butter in a saucepan. Add the eggs and cook gently, stirring all the time, until the eggs are scrambled and dry.

2. Pour in the consommé and gently heat up to the boiling point. Season to taste with salt and pepper.

3. Pour into soup bowls and allow to cool slightly before eating.

NOTE: You can dilute the consommé with a little water if the taste is too strong.

FROBSCOTTLE
FROM *THE BFG*

MAKES 4 TO 6 GLASSES

YOU WILL NEED:

blender or food processor
sieve

8 kiwi fruits, peeled
juice of 1 ½ limes
4 ounces raspberry drinking
  yogurt
8 ounces lemonade
12 ounces cream soda

1. Place the kiwis and lime juice in a blender or food processor and purée until liquified.

2. Push the mixture through a sieve. (A few seeds will escape, but this doesn't matter.)

3. Add the drinking yogurt and mix.

4. Gradually mix in the lemonade.

5. Pour in the cream soda, mix, and serve.

NOTE: If you wish to use ordinary yogurt instead of drinking yogurt, add it in step 1 and purée it along with the kiwis and lime juice.

CRISPY WASP STINGS ON A PIECE OF BUTTERED TOAST

FROM *JAMES AND THE GIANT PEACH*

SERVES 16

YOU WILL NEED:

small round cookie cutter
baking sheet
bowl

BUTTERED TOAST:

5 tablespoons unsalted butter,
softened
½ teaspoon cinnamon
4 slices white bread

WASP STINGS:

2 ½ ounces shredded coconut
¼ cup sifted confectioners' sugar
3 teaspoons honey or light corn
syrup
grated zest (yellow skin only) of
a quarter of a lemon

1. Work the butter and cinnamon together until thoroughly mixed.

2. Toast the bread. Cut four disks out of each slice and set aside.

3. Spread 2 ounces of the shredded coconut onto a baking sheet and sprinkle with the sifted confectioners' sugar.

4. Place under a hot broiler until the sugar begins to caramelize (it will happen very quickly), then with a spatula turn the coconut over and caramelize the underside.

5. Transfer to a bowl, add the honey and lemon zest, and mix well.

6. Add the remaining coconut.

7. Spread the cinnamon butter on the toast disks and top with the crispy wasp stings.

EATABLE
MARSHMALLOW PILLOWS
FROM *CHARLIE AND THE CHOCOLATE FACTORY*

SERVES 10 TO 15

YOU WILL NEED:

small and large saucepans
candy thermometer (optional)
large heatproof mixing bowl
electric beater
15 × 10 inch baking sheet
wax paper
piping bag with nozzle

MARSHMALLOW
PILLOWCASE:

6 tablespoons cold water
3 to 4 ounces gelatin
1 ¾ cups sugar
1 cup minus 3 tablespoons warm
   water
1 egg white, lightly beaten
a little oil (for greasing the
   baking sheet)
1 tablespoon cornstarch
¼ cup confectioners' sugar
7 ounces mini-marshmallows
decorating icing
various food colors or colored
   decorating icing

Start making this the day before serving to give the marshmallow time to dry out.

1. Pour the cold water into a small saucepan, sprinkle the gelatin on top, and set aside.

2. Place the sugar, warm water, and candy thermometer (if using) in a heavy-bottomed saucepan and stir gently over low heat until the sugar has dissolved.

3. Bring to a boil and let the mixture boil to 245°F, or until a little of the mixture dropped in cold water forms a firm ball. Remove from the heat and set aside.

4. Gently heat the gelatin over very low heat, stirring until dissolved. Do not allow it to boil.

5. Pour into a heatproof bowl (rinsed out with cold water to prevent the mixture from sticking). Gradually trickle the sugar syrup into the gelatin mixture, whisking continuously with the electric beater.

6. When the mixture is well thickened, beat in the egg white a little at a time, eventually making a marshmallow mixture. Continue until the mixture becomes very thick, resembling stiff meringue.

7. Pour the marshmallow mixture into the greased baking sheet and let set for 24 hours.

8. Mix together the cornstarch and confectioners' sugar. Dust a sheet of wax paper with the sugar mixture and turn out the set marshmallow pillowcase onto it.

9. Arrange the mini-marshmallows on one half of the pillowcase and fold the other half over to encase them, by folding the wax paper. Seal the edges with decorating icing.

10. Using the piping bag and decorating icing, create a frill for the pillow. Let dry.

Your pillow is now ready to decorate. Using food colors or colored icing, paint on stripes or the pattern of your choice. The possibilities are endless!

BOGGIS'S CHICKEN
FROM *FANTASTIC MR. FOX*

1. Put the chicken into a large saucepan with all the ingredients except the peas and the sauce and dumpling ingredients.

2. Add enough water to cover three-quarters of the chicken. Cover the pan with a well-fitting lid.

3. Bring to a boil gently, reduce the heat, and simmer gently until the chicken is cooked, about 1 ½ hours.

4. Remove the chicken from the pan and let cool. Strain the stock, reserving the carrots.

5. Skim off all the fat from the stock. Save 3 ¾ cups of the skimmed stock for the parsley sauce.

6. Remove the chicken skin and bone, and chop up the meat.

PARSLEY SAUCE:

7. In a large saucepan, melt the butter and add the flour. Stir and cook for 1 minute.

5 tablespoons butter
½ cup flour
2 cups milk
3 ¾ cups chicken stock
6 tablespoons chopped fresh
 parsley
salt and pepper

DUMPLINGS:

¾ cup all-purpose flour
1 teaspoon baking powder
2 ounces vegetable shortening or
 lard
2 ounces corn (optional)
½ teaspoon salt
a pinch of pepper
cold water

8. Combine the milk and chicken stock and gradually add to the butter-flour mixture. Bring to a boil, stirring continuously, cook for 1 minute, and remove from the heat. Stir in 5 ½ tablespoons of the parsley, and salt and pepper to taste.

DUMPLINGS:

9. Mix together the flour, baking powder, shortening, corn (if using), salt, and pepper. Bind with enough cold water to make a smooth dough. With floured hands, divide the dough into 12 portions and roll into balls.

10. Bring the sauce back to a simmer and add the chicken pieces, carrots, peas, and dumplings. (They will sink, but don't worry.)

11. Cover with a lid and cook for about 20 minutes, until the dumplings are light and fluffy.

12. Sprinkle with the remaining parsley and serve.

STICKJAW
FOR TALKATIVE PARENTS
FROM *CHARLIE AND THE CHOCOLATE FACTORY*

SERVES 10 TO 12

YOU WILL NEED:

piping bag and nozzle
baking sheet lined with baking
*   parchment*

2 egg whites
a pinch of salt
½ cup sugar
1 package toffee or caramel
*   candy, wrappers removed*
food coloring (optional)

1. Preheat oven to 250°F.

2. Whisk the egg whites and salt together until stiff.

3. Gradually whisk in the sugar until the meringue mixture is very stiff and shiny.

4. Spoon the meringue mixture into the piping bag (with the nozzle already in place).

5. Pipe a little meringue onto the lined sheet. Rest a candy on top and cover completely with more meringue, piping in the shape of a cone (see picture below).

6. Repeat until all the meringue is used up.

7. Bake for about 1 hour until dry and crisp. Remove from the oven and cool on a wire rack.

NOTE: You can color the meringue by adding a few drops of food coloring when whisking in the last of the sugar.

WILLY WONKA'S NUTTY CRUNCH SURPRISE
FROM *CHARLIE AND THE CHOCOLATE FACTORY*

SERVES 8

YOU WILL NEED:

Pyrex bowl
small saucepan
8 x 10 inch shallow pan
wax paper

7 ounces semisweet chocolate,
*   broken into small pieces*
4 tablespoons (½ stick) unsalted
*   butter*
5 tablespoons light corn syrup
3 ounces slivered almonds
6 plain vanilla cookies (Rich
*   Tea biscuits are good) or*
*   graham crackers, finely*
*   crushed*
1 ounce Rice Krispies
a few drops of vanilla extract

FOR THE NUTTY CRUNCH:

2 tablespoons water
½ cup sugar
2 ounces slivered almonds, finely
*   chopped*

1. Put the semisweet chocolate, butter, and corn syrup in a Pyrex bowl and place in a saucepan of simmering water. Stir occasionally until melted. (Or place the bowl in a microwave oven and cook on high for about 1 ½ minutes.)

2. Add the almonds, crushed cookies, Rice Krispies, and vanilla extract and mix well.

3. Spoon the mixture into a shallow pan lined with wax paper. Press the mixture down firmly with the back of a fork, creating a level surface.

4. Refrigerate until cool, then cut into bars.

5. Once the bars are ready, make the nutty crunch. Begin by placing the water and sugar in a small saucepan. Cook over low heat until the sugar has dissolved. Do not stir, but occasionally swirl the pan around gently. Once the sugar has dissolved, increase the heat and stir constantly until the sugar caramelizes and turns golden brown, about 2 to 3 minutes.

6. Remove from the heat. Working quickly, add the chopped almonds, stir thoroughly, and dip one end of each bar in the mixture. Place the bars on a sheet of buttered wax paper to set.

7. Melt the milk chocolate in a Pyrex bowl set in a saucepan of simmering water, or microwave as above.

Once it has melted, remove from the heat and dip the other end of each bar in the chocolate.

8. Let the bars cool on a sheet of wax paper.

HOT
ICE CREAM FOR COLD DAYS
FROM *CHARLIE AND THE CHOCOLATE FACTORY*

SERVES 6

YOU WILL NEED:

10-inch-square ovenproof dish, 2 inches deep

3 egg whites
a pinch of salt
¾ cup sugar
1 prepared spice cake
1 can (15 ounces) peach slices in syrup
1 quart good-quality vanilla ice cream (you probably won't use all of this)
stem ginger in syrup, drained and finely chopped (as little or as much as you dare)

1. Preheat the oven to 450°F.

2. Whisk the egg whites with the salt until stiff. Gradually whisk in the sugar until the meringue is very thick and shiny.

3. Cut the spice cake into three horizontal slices, then cut each slice into half.

4. Brush each piece of cake with a little peach syrup.

5. Arrange the six pieces in a square ovenproof dish.

6. Divide the peaches equally and place on top of the cake.

7. Mix the chopped slices of stem ginger into the meringue.

8. Carefully scoop the ice cream on top of the peaches (one scoop per piece of cake).

9. Spoon the meringue over the ice cream, completely covering the entire surface of the ice cream and the cake.

10. Place the dessert in the oven and bake until the meringue turns golden brown.

11. Serve immediately.

HAIR TOFFEE TO MAKE HAIR GROW ON BALD MEN
(FOR MOMS TO MAKE ONLY)
FROM *CHARLIE AND THE CHOCOLATE FACTORY*

YOU WILL NEED:

large heavy-bottomed saucepan
small greased pan or tray
candy thermometer (optional)
aluminum foil or plastic wrap

4 tablespoons (½ stick) unsalted
  butter
1 cup plus 2 tablespoons sugar
1 tablespoon warm water
1 tablespoon white wine vinegar
2 tablespoons light corn syrup
4 ounces egg vermicelli, broken
  in half and cooked

1. Melt the butter in a large heavy-bottomed saucepan, stir in the sugar, and remove the pan from the heat.

2. Add the water, vinegar, and corn syrup, and stir over low heat until the sugar dissolves. *Do not* allow the mixture to boil.

3. Add the egg vermicelli.

4. Place the candy thermometer (if using) into the pan.

5. Now bring the mixture to a boil and boil steadily for about 15 to 20 minutes, or until the thermometer reads 305°F.

6. Pour the toffee into the greased pan and let it cool. As soon as it is cool enough to handle, lightly grease your hands with butter. Take two forks and scrape up some toffee with a few strands of vermicelli in it. Then, using your hands, roll the toffee into a small bite-size mound. Repeat.

7. Place on a greased tray and allow to set.

8. Wrap and twist individually in plastic wrap or aluminum foil to prevent them from becoming sticky.

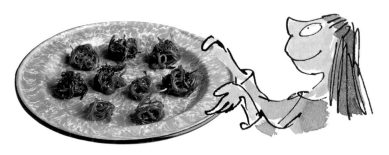

The late **Roald Dahl** was one of the most beloved storytellers of all time. His many popular children's books include *Charlie and the Chocolate Factory, James and the Giant Peach,* and *Matilda.*

Quentin Blake has drawn ever since he can remember. In addition to illustrating more than a dozen of Roald Dahl's books, he has collaborated with such well-known authors as Joan Aiken and Russell Hoban, and has written and illustrated his own picture books.